YOU GOT OLDER

YOU GOT OLDER

⊰ A PLAY ⊱

CLARE BARRON

NORTHWESTERN UNIVERSITY PRESS

EVANSTON, ILLINOIS

Northwestern University Press
www.nupress.northwestern.edu

Printed in the United States of America

10 9 8 7 6 5 4 3 2 1

LIBRARY OF CONGRESS
CATALOGING-IN-PUBLICATION DATA

Names: Barron, Clare, author.
Title: You got older : a play / Clare Barron.
Description: Evanston, Illinois : Northwestern University Press, 2017. | "You Got Older, by Clare Barron, received its world premiere on October 29, 2014, with Page 73 Productions (Liz Jones and Asher Richelli, Executive Directors; Michael Walkup, Producing Director). The production took place at HERE Arts Center in New York City. It was directed by Anne Kauffman." | Includes bibliographical references.
Identifiers: LCCN 2016052822 | ISBN 9780810135284 (pbk. : alk. paper) | ISBN 9780810135291 (e-book)
Subjects: LCSH: Families—Drama. | Cancer—Patients—Family relationships—Drama. | Fathers and daughters—Drama.
Classification: LCC PS3602.A837246 Y68 2017 | DDC 812/.6—dc23
LC record available at https://lccn.loc.gov/ 2016052822

CONTENTS

NOTES FROM THE PLAYWRIGHT

This play was written and finished in the middle of a personal crisis—before anything was resolved. And so, for me, it remains a kind of play *without* perspective. The characters are so far inside of something that they don't know how to explain what's happening to them. The result is a lot of avoidance. Avoidance through sex, avoidance through celebration, avoidance through logistics and banality and worrying about other things . . . Emotions spring up in strange places. Thoughts are half-processed, and there's a desire to talk about something "meaningful" more than there is a knowledge of what to say.

Being intimate with our families is a terrifying thing. And it's particularly terrifying to be intimate with *our parents*. There are so many dark and perverse parts of us that we have to keep hidden even as we desire to be close. And besides, there's no real way across the chasm anyway. We're all doomed to our private lives and our private suffering. *Do you know what I mean?*

With this in mind, the play (for me) is as much about the things shared as it is about all the things left unsaid. And my perhaps optimistic belief that there's profound comfort to be found just in living privately together. Life and desire can persist even if all we can muster up is the courage and time to sit together with something unspeakable between us.

On Notation

Punctuation is not grammatical. It is capricious, emotional and, most importantly, rhythmic.

For example, the lines:

"Oh, I don't know" and "Oh I don't know"

. . . have two different rhythms.

When a character's section of dialogue ends with a period, that indicates a stuck landing—a slight emphasis or the end of a thought. When a character's section of dialogue ends with no punctuation, keep the text rolling.

Text that is formatted poetically with line breaks indicates a slight suspension between each line. But you can play with it like poetry, sometimes choosing to roll over the break.

A slash (/) indicates overlapping dialogue.

To borrow from the playwright Kristen Kosmas: "Play it like music."

On Songs

Dad's theme song is "Firewood" by Regina Spektor. The wedding song at the very end of the play is "Timber" by Pitbull (feat. Ke$ha). Both of those moments were born out of those specific songs, and so I think they're perfect.

"Why Was She Born So Beautiful" is an English rugby song. You can find it online.

PRODUCTION HISTORY

You Got Older, by Clare Barron, received its world premiere on October 29, 2014, with Page 73 Productions (Liz Jones and Asher Richelli, Executive Directors; Michael Walkup, Producing Director). The production took place at HERE Arts Center in New York City. It was directed by Anne Kauffman, with sets by Daniel Zimmerman, costumes by Ásta Bennie Hostetter, lights by Russell Champa, composition and sound by Daniel Kluger, props by Deb Gaouette, fight direction by Jeff Barry, and casting by Jack Doulin and Sharky. The production manager was Dennis O'Leary-Gullo, and the stage manager was Sonja Thorson. *You Got Older* was originally developed in the Soho Rep Writer/ Director Lab (Sarah Benson, Artistic Director; Cynthia Flowers, Executive Director).

The cast of the New York production was as follows:

Mae . . . . .Brooke Bloom
Dad . . . . Reed Birney
Cowboy. . . . . .Michael Schantz
Mac. . . . . .William Jackson Harper
Matthew . . . . Ted Schneider
Jenny. . . . . .Keilly McQuail
Hannah . . . . Miriam Silverman

YOU GOT OLDER

CHARACTERS

Mae, thirty-two

Dad, father of Mae, in his sixties

Cowboy, you don't know if he's gonna fuck you or kill you

Mac, a dude from Mae's hometown, thirty-four

Matthew, middle brother

Jenny, little sister

Hannah, big sister

Nurse, can be played by Cowboy

[*A vegetable garden. Little mounds of dirt. And vegetables propped up with sticks. It's late summer. Everything feels very far away from us. Or very—uncomfortably—close.* MAE *and* DAD *stand over the vegetables.* DAD *has a scar that goes across his neck from one ear to the other ear. It looks like someone tried to cut his head off.*]

DAD: So these are our peppers

MAE: They're green

DAD: Yup

MAE: I thought they were going to be red

DAD: No. They're green peppers

MAE: Are they spicy?

DAD: No they're sweet.
Try one

[MAE *tries a pepper.*]

MAE: What are you going to do with them?

DAD: Oh I don't know. Salads. I haven't really thought about it

MAE: That's exciting that you're growing vegetables

DAD: Yes

MAE: What other things are you going to grow?

DAD: Just peppers for now. And these leafy green things. I don't know what they are

MAE: Mustard greens?

DAD: No

MAE: Collards?

DAD: No. It's more unusual than that

MAE: Swiss chard?

DAD: It starts with an "A"

[MAE *thinks.*]

MAE: I don't know any greens that start with the letter "A"

DAD: I'm pretty sure it starts with the letter "A." Like *amethyst.*

MAE: I don't know it.

DAD: I take about six leaves with me sometimes when I pack a lunch and I just eat them raw.

[MAE *and* DAD *stand in the yard.*]

MAE: Is that a fire pit?

DAD: Yes.

MAE: Where did it come from?

DAD: I made it.

MAE: Why did you make a fire pit?

[*He shrugs.*]

DAD: I was feeling industrious

MAE: Do you have fires?

DAD: I've had one fire. To test it out

MAE: How did it work?

DAD: It worked good

MAE: Can we have a fire?

DAD: We can if you want. We just have to get some firewood

[MAE *picks up a stick in the yard.*]

MAE: What about this?

[*He feels the stick.*]

DAD: I think it's too wet to burn.
    We've been having a lot of wet days, recently.
    I think tomorrow is supposed to be wet, too.

MAE: Is it?

DAD: That's what I heard

[MAE *and* DAD *stand in the yard.*]

DAD: Do you still need to go to the pharmacy?

MAE: Yeah, if you don't mind

DAD: What do you need? Maybe we have it

MAE: No I checked. You don't have it

DAD: Are you sure? There's a whole stockpile of things down in the laundry room

MAE: I need a toothbrush

DAD: We have toothbrushes

MAE: I like a certain kind of toothbrush

DAD: We have all kinds of toothbrushes. Your mother was like a squirrel. I'm still finding things she ferreted away

MAE: I like soft bristles

DAD: We have soft bristles

MAE: Yeah everyone has soft bristles. I don't know who buys hard bristles. Or medium bristles

DAD: I sometimes buy medium bristles

MAE: Dad! Don't do that! You should always buy soft bristles. They're better for your gums

DAD: We have bad gums in our family

MAE: I know

DAD: Receding gums

MAE: I know. My dentist told me

DAD: I'm sorry about that

MAE: It's okay

DAD: And gingivitis

MAE: I know

DAD: I think in general we have very acidic mouths

MAE: I think so too

[*Little pause.*]

DAD: So soft bristles

MAE: Uh-huh. And also my dentist recommended that I get a child-sized toothbrush

DAD: Really

MAE: Because I have a small mouth

DAD: That's a clever idea

MAE: He said that a child-sized toothbrush would fit better in my mouth and it would be easier for me to clean all the crevices of my teeth, especially in the back of my mouth

DAD: I bet that's true

MAE: I don't know. That's what he told me.

DAD: So we'll buy you a toothbrush

MAE: Also I need to pick up a prescription

DAD: A prescription?

MAE: Yeah, they called it in from Minneapolis

DAD: That was nice of them

MAE: Yeah but it was supposed to be there this morning and I called them and they didn't have it in yet

DAD: How come they didn't have it?

MAE: I don't know. I thought it was a normal thing but I guess it wasn't

DAD: What kind of drug is it?

MAE: It's not a drug. It's an ointment. It's a prescription ointment

DAD: Did they have to overnight it?

MAE: I guess

DAD: That's what they do. They overnight it. Whenever they don't have it in stock they just overnight it from Seattle

MAE: And what if Seattle doesn't have it?

DAD: I think Seattle always has it

MAE: Yeah well I hope Seattle has it. I'm supposed to get a text message telling me it's ready to be picked up

DAD: You get a text message from the pharmacy?

MAE: Yeah they text me

DAD: The pharmacist texts you?

MAE: Not personally. It's an automated thing

DAD: Do you have to pay for that?

MAE: I get free texts

DAD: That's good

MAE: Well, not *free* texts. But I don't pay per text

DAD: Well that's still pretty cool

MAE: Except they haven't texted me yet. So I don't know whether to go or whether we should wait for the text

DAD: Maybe you should call them to see if they got it—

MAE: Ugh. I don't want to call them—

DAD: So you don't go all the way down there, if they don't have it in yet

MAE: Why wouldn't they have it in?

DAD: I don't know

MAE: That would really suck

DAD: Is it urgent?

MAE: I mean, it's urgent. But it's not *that* urgent.

DAD: If it's urgent, I can drive you to Seattle

MAE: It's not urgent. I just wish they would text me

DAD: Why don't you call them?

[MAE *and* DAD *stand in the yard. They look at the peppers. They look at the fire pit. They look at the sky.*]

    I put you in Hannah's room. I hope that's okay

MAE: Oh.

DAD: It felt strange to have you sleeping in the basement with only two of us in the house

MAE: I like the basement

DAD: I can put you in the basement

MAE: No Hannah's room is fine. It's cheerful

DAD: Good

[MAE *smiles.*]

MAE: We'll be right next to each other.

•◆•

[MAE *wakes up in bed. It's snowing outside. There's a strange man in the corner. He kind of looks like a Canadian cowboy.*]

MAE: Where am I?

COWBOY: Nova Scotia

MAE: Is it snowing?

COWBOY: There's a blizzard

MAE: A blizzard?!

COWBOY: Yup. It's blizzarding.

[MAE *looks out the window of the cabin. It's blizzarding outside.*]

I found you tied to a tree.

MAE: What?

COWBOY: You were buried halfway in the snow. Unconscious. Your mouth was open. There were snowflakes on your tongue.

MAE: Who would have tied me to a tree?

COWBOY: You tell me

[MAE *tries to think of who would want to tie her to the tree in the middle of a blizzard but she can't think of anyone. Suddenly she realizes. . .*]

MAE: Hey. Am I naked?

COWBOY: I had to take your clothes off so you wouldn't freeze to death. I'm sorry. I didn't look

MAE: Um. Can I have them back?

COWBOY: They're still wet. I'm drying them by the fire

MAE: I have to go to the bathroom

[COWBOY *strides across the room. He sets a pot next to the bed and retreats.*]

COWBOY: There's no toilet

MAE: Oh.
  Maybe I'll wait.

COWBOY: It's going to be a while

[MAE *hesitates. Then she climbs out of the bed, using the sheet as a bathrobe. She squats over the pot. She pees. It's so cold that her piss produces steam. She pushes the pot under the bed out of view. She climbs back into bed, still wearing the sheet, and gets under the covers. She lies very still.*]

MAE: Hey. What's your name?

COWBOY: Daryl. No. Luke. My name is Luke

MAE: Hey Luke. If there's a blizzard, does that mean we're trapped?

[COWBOY *is standing over the bed.*]

COWBOY: I have to rub you down now

MAE: . . .

COWBOY: You're hypothermic

MAE: . . .

COWBOY: The friction will warm you up

MAE: Please don't

COWBOY: Rub you down?

MAE: Yes. Don't do that. Please

COWBOY: I'm sorry. I don't have a choice. It's for your own good

MAE: Can't I just do it myself?

COWBOY: Mae?

MAE: How do you know my name?

COWBOY: I'm going to rub you down now.
    Even if I have to tie you to that bed
    I am going to rub
    Every part
    Of your body
    Vigorously
    Until heat
    And feeling
    return
    to every
    part
    of
    yer
    body.

MAE: . . .

COWBOY: Don't look at the door.
    There's a blizzard outside, remember?
    You're not going anywhere.

[*The door opens.* DAD *enters.*]

DAD [*full of exuberance*]: Hey Mae! We've got another pepper!

[*He sees* MAE *naked in bed.*]

    Oh sorry!

MAE: No it's fine. I'm just sleeping. Thinking. Sleeping. I'm just about to get up

DAD: Well when you're ready come out and I'll show you the new pepper.

[DAD *exits, leaving* MAE *alone with* COWBOY LUKE.]

•◆•

[DAD *and* MAE *sit in the yard around the empty fire pit. They are next to the peppers. There is a baby new one.*]

MAE: This is almost like we're camping

DAD: Yeah

MAE: We don't even have to go hiking anymore we can just come out here

DAD: No views though

MAE: I don't really care about the views

[*They sit in silence.*]

Are you going into the office this afternoon?

DAD: Nah, I think I'll just send some emails from home.

[*They sit.*]

MAE: It didn't rain

DAD: No

MAE: I don't think it's going to rain today either

DAD: I don't think so either

MAE: Maybe we can make a fire

[*They sit in silence.*]

DAD: The thing that always gets me is this. You're outside. You're looking at the sky. And it's a beautiful sky. You're happy to be alive. You're aware that you're having a nice moment. That it's a good moment in your life. But then how long should you let it go on, you know? Shouldn't you just look at the sky forever? Or at the very least until you get very hungry and you have to go do something else? But I'm always itching to go do something else even when I'm in the middle of having a nice moment. It makes me feel guilty.

[*They sit.* MAE *thinks about Damian, whom she fucked without a condom even though she didn't really want to fuck him without a condom, and how she put her legs over his shoulders. Or his legs over her . . . ? No. His shoulders. Her legs over his shoulders.*]

MAE: Should we go in?

• ◆ •

[MAE *out at Hank's Saloon. A dingy local bar. She drinks a beer. A smallish guy sits one stool over. He keeps checking* MAE *out.*]

MAC: Hey

MAE: Hey

MAC: Do I know you?

MAE: No

MAC: I think I know you

MAE: I don't think so

MAC: Washington Elementary School?

MAE: Yes

MAC: Mrs. Armstrong's fourth-grade class?

MAE: Yes

MAC: Mac. I mean, I was Malcolm then. But now I'm Mac

MAE: Oh. Oh! Oh I think I remember you! Sorry. I totally remember you. Mrs. Armstrong! Yes!

MAC: It's okay. How are you doing?

MAE: Fine. How are you?

MAC: I'm good, I'm good
    Are you living / here?

MAE: Visiting. I'm visiting

MAC: Cool

MAE: Yeah

    . . .

    . . .

    Actually I'm not fine. Actually I'm awful.

MAC: Oh?

MAE: Yeah. I'm actually having like the worst moment of my life right now. Well almost the worst. [*Thinking.*] Like the second worst moment of my life so far.

MAC: I'm sorry

MAE: Yeah. My dad has cancer

MAC: Oh no

MAE: Like really bad cancer

MAC: What kind of cancer?

MAE [*on a roll*]: Like weird, mysterious cancer that had spread all over
his body but they couldn't find the primary source and it turns
out that the primary source was only three millimeters big and in
his larynx even though he doesn't smoke and doesn't drink and
doesn't have HPV (I'm pretty sure) and he had to go to Seattle
and have this surgery with robots and now he looks like someone
tried to chop his head off

MAC: Oh my god

MAE: Yeah and they made him get chemo and radiation and stuff but
they didn't want to surgically remove his larynx, obviously, so
now he has to go *back* to Seattle to get his larynx zapped directly
with this high-powered radiation laser proton—

MAC: Jesus

MAE: —knife thing-y and then he's done

MAC: Well that's good

MAE: And also this dude who was like the love of my life dumped me
And he was my boss
So he fired me

MAC: He fired you?

MAE: So I don't have a job anymore
Or health insurance

MAC: Is that legal?

MAE: Or an *apartment*
And my little sister has a pericardial cyst

MAC: What?

MAE [*to herself*]: He didn't really "fire me." I shouldn't have said that . . .

MAC: Wait. Your sister has what?

MAE: Like a cyst in her heart that's been growing since she was born

MAC: Oh my god is she going to be okay?

MAE: I mean, she had to have heart surgery but it was like noninvasive heart surgery. / They just stuck a needle in her

MAC: Oh my god

MAE: She's totally fine. Apparently it's like a totally normal—

MAC: Heart cysts?

MAE: Yeah, but of course she's *freaking out* about it because of my dad. And because of my mom.

MAC: What's wrong with your mom?

MAE: Uh. My mom is deceased

MAC: Oh shit

MAE: It's okay. It happened a while ago. I was in college

MAC: I'm surprised I didn't know about it

[MAE *shrugs.*]

MAE: I don't know. Did you know my mom?

MAC: I mean, I know *you*. I probably met your mom

   . . .

   . . .

   Well, I'm sorry to hear about / all your—

MAE: Sorry. I don't mean to yak your ear off

MAC: No you're not—

MAE: I'm just going crazy at home
    And I'm horny as hell
    It's like
    I haven't had sex in . . .

[*She counts.*]

    forty-one days
    And now I'm at home
    with my dad
    Sleeping in a *bedroom* next to his *bedroom*
    And he's always barging in all the time
    To talk to me about peppers
    And I just like
    Needed a drink
    And some space to think
    dirty thoughts

MAC: . . .
    You know. I always had the biggest crush on you

MAE: Really?

MAC: Yeah.

MAE: Weren't we like in fourth grade?

MAC: I don't know. It just stayed with me. All through high school

[MAE *drinks her beer.*]

    Does your dad know you're here?

[MAE *grins*.]

MAE: I snuck out

MAC: Whoa. Sneaky lady

MAE: It was my first time sneaking out

MAC: Really?

MAE: Yeah. I've never done that before. I was a really good kid

MAC: Never?

MAE: I used to sneak boys *in*. I used to sneak boys *in* and then fool around with them until four in the morning with my parents sleeping upstairs. I used to live in the basement

MAC: That's hot

MAE: It wasn't that hot

MAC: It sounds pretty hot

MAE: It felt hot at the time but I'm not sure anymore if it was actually that hot

[*She drinks her beer.*]

I used to have a fantasy where my high school boyfriend Dave Gellatly—who totally cheated on me and like destroyed all of my self-confidence—would come to my window and knock on my window and then I would let him in and then he would be high on cocaine (even though I'm pretty sure he never did cocaine) and he would like rape me? And the whole time I'm thinking: Maybe I should scream! If I scream, my parents will wake up and come down here and save me and this whole thing will stop. But then if my parents come down here, they'll see me naked with Dave on top of me. And I'm like a virgin. And super Christian. So I don't scream. Because I'm too embarrassed. And he rapes me. And then later I decide to report it. And the whole town vilifies me and I'm like this outcast woman? And then Dave dies in a drunk driving accident and everyone is like: If you had just not reported it he would have *died* anyway and you would've gotten justice without having to besmirch his name.

MAC: That was a fantasy?

MAE: I guess I just used to think about it when I needed to cry

[MAE *drinks her beer.*]

MAC: I know Dave

MAE: You do?

MAC: Yeah. Not that well. We were on the soccer team together for a year

MAE: Well, that's embarrassing.

. . .

Don't tell him about that

MAC: I won't

MAE: He already thinks I'm crazy

MAC: I never see him. Don't worry

MAE: Okay. I'm going to go

MAC: Let me buy you a drink

MAE: I'm tired

MAC: Whatever you want

MAE: Another time

MAC: . . .

   You don't like me

MAE: No I like you

MAC: Just tell me if you don't like me

MAE: I like you

MAC: Just say it

MAE: I like you, Mac

MAC: Say it to my face. Say it to me

MAE: I—

MAC: Say it

MAE: . . .

   I don't like you

MAC: There. You said it.

MAE: I don't like you

MAC: Okay

MAE: I don't like you

MAC: I got it

MAE: I don't like you
   I don't like you

      . . .

   I'm lying.
   I like you.
   I'd like to have sex with you tonight.

MAC: You'd like to have sex with me tonight?

MAE: But I have a rash.

MAC: You have a rash?

MAE: On my back. From here [*pointing to the top of her back, her shoulders*] to here [*pointing to the bottom of her back, just above her ass*]

MAC: Okay

MAE: And also under my boob.
So I can't have sex.
I feel too self-conscious.
I finally got this ointment in from Seattle
But it hasn't cleared it up yet

MAC: How did you get your rash?

MAE: I don't know. Dairy? I don't know. Maybe stress. Maybe HIV.

MAC: . . .

MAE: One day I just woke up in the middle of the night with this itch right in the middle of my back. And it was weird. But somehow my brain didn't register that it was *weird* weird. So I just went on with life and never looked at my back. And then one night I was having sex with my boyfriend and we hadn't had sex in a long time and he said: "Oh my god. Look at your back." And it was a rash from here [*pointing to the top of her back*] to here [*pointing to the bottom of her back, just above her ass*]. It had spread! And Ian was like: "It's fine. Let's keep having sex." But I was like: "No. Let's do it another time." And then the rash never cleared up. It just stayed. And we didn't have sex. And then we broke up. Not because of the rash or anything. It was just weird timing.

[*She considers this, then leans in like she's saying something really top secret.*]

But I think maybe they were related? Like maybe the rash was my subconscious's way of telling me that we needed to break up?

MAC: What does it look like?

MAE: . . .

MAC: Is it like—hives? Or—

MAE: A thousand little bumps that feel like bumpy little lines. Like bumpy little mountain ranges that run from my neck to my ass. And the mountains are red. And pus-y.

MAC: Can I see it?

MAE: No!

MAC: Let me see it!

MAE: There are only two people in this world who I would let see my back in a state like this and one of them is my sister and you are not the other

MAC: . . .
  I like pus
  I like things like that
  I like scabs
  And ingrown hairs
  And flaky skin
  I like to pick at things
  I'm serious
  I won't judge you
  It'll probably make me like you even more

MAE: . . .

MAC: I had an ingrown hair in my armpit once
  And the amount of pus that came out of it . . .
  It was like squeezing toothpaste out of a tube

MAE: I like chewing beard hairs

MAC: Really?

MAE: Yeah. I like plucking beard hairs from guys' faces
    And then chewing on them

MAC: I like chewing on toenails

MAE: My ex-boyfriend used to let me pluck out beard hairs with my
    teeth

MAC: You can pluck one of my beard hairs with your teeth

MAE: Really?

MAC: If you let me see your rash

[MAE *considers the trade.*]

MAE: Okay

[*She moves her mouth toward his cheek.*]

    It hurts a little

MAC: That's okay

[*She moves her mouth towards his cheek. She stops herself.*]

MAE: Some people don't like it

MAC: I bet I'll like it

MAE: Just don't get mad at me, if you don't like it

MAC: Whatever happens
    I won't get mad
    I promise

[MAE *puts her mouth on* MAC's *cheek. She finds a thick, juicy hair
with her tongue. She seizes the hair with her two front teeth. She pulls*

gently away from MAC's *face. His cheek skin stretches. Then* *pop*! *The hair comes out.* MAE *chews on the hair.*]

MAE: I just love the texture.

[MAE *chews the hair.* MAC *lets her enjoy this.*]

MAC: Okay. Now let me see your rash

MAE: . . .

MAC: . . .

MAE: Just for a second

MAC: Just for a second

MAE: Please be kind

MAC: I will

MAE: Don't think I'm disgusting

MAC: I would never think anyone, *anyone* with a rash is disgusting

[MAE *lifts up her shirt and shows* MAC *her bare back.*]

Oooooooooh

MAE: What?!

MAC: That looks painful

MAE: It itches

MAC: I'm just going to touch it very softly with my fingertips, is that okay?

[MAC *touches* MAE's *rash very softly with his fingertips.*]

MAE: That feels good

MAC: Good

[MAC *lightly touches* MAE's *rash.*]

MAE: Actually, um. Can I ask you a huge favor?

MAC: Sure

MAE: Do you mind putting ointment on it? It's just I can never reach the middle of my back. And I don't want to ask my dad

MAC: No totally

MAE: You don't mind?

MAC: Give me the ointment

[MAE *gives* MAC *the ointment. He smears it on her back.*]

MAE: Are you getting it everywhere?

MAC: Yes

MAE: Are you putting enough on? You have to put a lot on

MAC: Your back is smothered in ointment

[MAC *blows on* MAE's *ointment covered back.*]

MAE: Oh my god
    That feels so good
    It's minty fresh on my back

[*He lowers her shirt.*]

    Thank you

MAC: No problem

MAE: Okay. I should go

[*She gathers her things.*]

MAC: Hey so what's your job?

MAE: Sorry?

MAC: The job you lost?
    What do you do?
    What are you?

MAE: I'm a lawyer. In Minneapolis

MAC: Oh. Wow

MAE: Yeah. It's embarrassing

MAC: No it's not. It's impressive
    I always pictured you making jam somewhere

MAE: Really?

MAC: Yeah, I always pictured you selling hams and jams and nectar-
    ines somewhere on the side of the highway. You know. Future
    Farmers of America

MAE: Huh?

MAC: Remember? Future Farmers of America?

MAE: Oh.
    Oh.
    You're thinking of my sister—

MAC: What?

MAE: You're thinking of my sister Hannah
    I'm not Hannah

I'm Mae
Hannah's little sister

MAC: Oh!

MAE: Yeah Hannah was all up in FFA
And Hannah and I were both in Mrs. Armstrong's fourth-grade
class
And Hannah lives in Boise and teaches Special Education, so not
strawberry jam or anything but yeah

MAC: Oh shit

MAE: So yeah. I was right. I don't remember you

MAC: I'm so sorry

MAE: No it's okay

MAC: I feel so stupid

MAE: Oh my god. I feel so much better

MAC: I'm such an idiot. / Jesus Christ

MAE: The whole time I was sitting here going crazy thinking I don't
know who the fuck this is. I felt like such an asshole.

MAC: . . .

MAE: . . .
Well. I'm going to go
Nice to meet you, Mac

MAC: Nice to meet you, Mae

MAE: I'll tell my sister you say hi

MAC: You don't have to do that

[MAE *heads to the door.*]

Oh! You forgot your—

[*He holds up the paper prescription bag with the ointment in it.*]

MAE: Oh

MAC: Hold up

[MAC *takes out a pen and writes his number on the bag. He hands it to* MAE.]

That's my number

MAE: Haha

MAC: Call me, if you get bored
     Or you need a break from your dad or whatever
     I've got a pretty sweet place
     And . . . a pretty sweet cat
     Murphy
     He's—
     He sleeps with me
     He's pretty sweet
     He doesn't *have* to sleep with me, I mean—
     I'm just
     I'm just joking

MAE: Sounds fun

MAC: How long you in town for?

MAE: I'm not sure
     Maybe till the end of summer?
     Maybe till my dad finishes treatment and then—
     I'm not sure

MAC: It's going to be fall soon

MAE: Yup

MAC: It always sneaks up on me

MAE: Me too

MAC: And then after fall, it's going to be Christmas

•◆•

[*The leaves fall off the trees. Torrential rain.* MAE *and* DAD *stand inside at the window, staring at the garden, the leaves on the ground, the naked trees . . . It thunders. The rain comes down even harder.*]

MAE: The fire pit is going to be wet for weeks.

[*They stare at the rain.*]

DAD: So Matthew's flying in

MAE: Uh-huh

DAD: And Hannah's already there, I think. She wanted to get everything settled for you guys. And Jenny's driving up tomorrow morning

MAE: Cool

DAD: They've got her on the night shift. I told her not to come, but—

MAE: Jenny's crazy

DAD: She doesn't want to be the only one who's not there.
So! Very nice
All of you
For your dad
Very nice children

[MAE *laughs.*]

MAE: Dad

DAD: What? It's true
Very nice children
You are

[*They stare at the rain.*]

MAE: Are you nervous?

DAD: No

MAE: It's okay to be nervous

DAD: Why should I be nervous? I don't have to do anything. I just
have to lie there

MAE: That's worse, don't you think?

DAD: No

MAE: I think it's worse to not have control

DAD: If I were in charge of it, we'd all be in trouble

MAE: I just mean I hate it when I feel helpless

DAD: Not me. I love it.

MAE: Stop. You do not.

DAD: I do. I love it. I love it when you just get to lie back and let
people take care of you . . .
Like going to the dentist
I love that
You just lie back and open your mouth
What can you do?

[They stare at the rain. DAD *absentmindedly fingers his scar.* MAE *watches him.]*

MAE: You want to know something funny? I have a lump. In the same exact place that you found your lump

DAD: You do?

MAE: Yeah, isn't that crazy? I've had it for years

DAD: Mae! Did you get it checked out?

MAE: Yeah, it's no big deal. They said it's an enlarged salivary gland. Lots of people have them

DAD: Well good

MAE: It's like my little sympathy lump, you know? Like when people get sympathy pregnant? And feel like they're pregnant? Even though they're not? Except I've had it since before we found out you had cancer

DAD: Well I've had cancer since before we found out I had cancer, too

[They stare at the rain, both fingering their necks.]

Oh, don't let me forget. I have a present for you from Tiffany

MAE: Wait, who's Tiffany?

DAD: Tiffany at the office. You know / Tiffany. She knit you a blanket

MAE: Oh, yeah!
Why did she knit me a blanket???

DAD: Tiffany is always knitting everybody blankets. She likes it
Besides, hospitals are cold.

MAE: I know

DAD: She knit me one too

    . . .

Maybe you should do some knitting again

MAE: Dad

DAD: Didn't you used to knit?

MAE: Sometimes

DAD: I don't know. It could be something to do while you're here. Keep yourself busy. Even in moments of transition. It's important to keep yourself busy.

MAE: I know

DAD: I'm pretty sure we've still got somebody's yarn down in the basement . . .

[*They stare at the rain.*]

At some point, I'm going to ask you some questions you probably don't want me to ask you. About your plans. For the future

MAE: Oh no

DAD: Not now. Just at some point we should talk about what your next steps are

MAE: Dad. I don't know my next steps

DAD: Not right now!

MAE: I don't know when I'm going to know my next steps

DAD: Well at some point, I'm going to bug you

MAE: . . .

DAD: How's Ian doing anyway?

MAE: I have no idea. I don't talk to Ian

DAD: You know. Whenever I like them, it's the kiss of death

MAE: Oh come on

DAD: I'm serious. It's true. Who did I like? I liked Johnny. And look what happened to him and Hannah!

MAE: Dad. That had nothing to do with you

DAD: Who else did I like? I liked Carlos. I *really* liked Carlos. And Stephanie. And Ashley. They're all gone!

MAE: You like Michael, don't you? He's still around

DAD: Michael's alright.
From now on, only date people I hate

MAE: You should hate Ian!

DAD: I don't know. I thought you two were really good together

MAE: Mom always hated the people I broke up with
She referred to Austin as the Big A-Hole for years

DAD: She was just pretending. She and Austin used to send each other Christmas letters

MAE: Well I'd appreciate it if you'd at least pretend

[*They stare at the rain.*]

You know Kimber?

DAD: No

MAE: Orchestra Kimber? She played the / bassoon

DAD: Oh yes. I always liked Kimber. She was one of my favorites

MAE: I know

DAD: She just seemed a lot more spunky than the rest of your friends

MAE: I know

DAD: I like it when girls are spunky

MAE: Her dad is sick. Some inoperable, terminal cancer

DAD: Oh dear

MAE: Whatever we don't have to go into it but she's always posting things about faith and family on her Facebook wall. And how Jesus is testing her family. And how fire is necessary to make the forest grow. And everything happens for a reason. Stuff like that.

DAD: Yeah

MAE: And normally I hate that stuff. Normally I *hate* that stuff. But the other day I was thinking how funny it is that my life fell apart. And then all this happened to you.

DAD: It's not that funny.

MAE: Well. Not funny. But convenient

[*They stare at the rain. It turns into snow. A terrible snowstorm. Lightning, thunder. A thundersnow.* MAE *is staggering through the snow. She calls out for help but we can't hear her above the noise of the storm. She collapses.*]

[COWBOY *appears. He digs her out of a snowdrift and hefts her with one hand onto his shoulder. He trudges through the storm—back inside—and throws her onto the floor in a wet, cold heap. She shivers.*]

MAE: Thank you

COWBOY: You almost got yourself killed

MAE: I'm sorry

COWBOY: You almost got me killed going after you

[*They both sit on the floor, panting.*]

    Come here

[*She does.*]

    Get down

MAE: Why?

COWBOY: On the floor

[*She does. He takes out a long, thick rope from a pouch on his thigh.*]

MAE: What are you doing?

COWBOY: Making sure you don't run away again

[*He starts to tie her up: wrist-to-ankle, wrist-to-ankle.*]

    You act like a child, I'm going to treat you like a child

MAE: You tie your children up like this?

[MAE *is thoroughly tied up.*]

COWBOY: Can you move?

MAE [*trying to move*]: No

[COWBOY *steps aside. Lights a cigarette.*]

COWBOY: Are you cold?

[MAE *shrugs*.]

MAE: I'm wet

COWBOY: I can hold you if you're cold

[MAE *lets him hold her. It feels* so good *to be held. She relaxes into him*.]

MAE: There was this person, um
 My boyfriend. Ian
 And the last time we had sex
 We were on my floor
 On top of all my dirty clothes
 And we just fucked
 No foreplay
 Or anything
 And then he flipped around
 He was trying to make me cum, and I was just lying there . . .
 Staring out past his ass crack, you know
 Out at the sky
 Out at the tree outside my window
 And his ass in my face
 And I was just looking at that tree
 And the sky was blue
 And the tree was like a crack across the sky
 And I was so sad. Like: Is this it? Is this all there is? But also: This
 is enough, you know. It felt like enough.
 . . .
 . . .
 . . .
 Is it lonely? Being a cowboy?

COWBOY: I've always been alone. It's in my nature

MAE: Well maybe I'm a cowboy, too . . .

[COWBOY *puffs his cigarette.*]

Give me some of that

[*He offers it to her, placing it delicately between her lips. She inhales and blows smoke into his face.*]

COWBOY: Mae. Are you trying to get me to kiss you?

MAE: Maybe

COWBOY: If I kiss you, I might not be able to stop

[*This is the best thing that anybody has said to* MAE *in a very, very long time.*]

MAE: I think that's, um
    I think that's fine

[MAE *props herself up. Their two heads veer toward each other.* MAE *reaches out to grab his big, thick jaw and sees something on his neck. She recoils.*]

MAE: What's that?

COWBOY: What?

MAE: On your neck?

COWBOY: It's a sore spot

MAE: A sore spot?

COWBOY: Yeah, I've got a whole line of them

[*He unbuttons his shirts to reveal a big, red, angry line of weeping lesions down his neck to his stomach and on toward his groin.*]

I don't know, I think they're boils?
Or some kind of—

[*He coughs. An awful hacking cough.*]

Sorry. Lesions

[*There's blood all over his hands.*]

[*A light comes on in the hallway. The sound of coughing.* DAD *up in the middle of the night.*]

MAE [*calling out*]: Dad? You okay?

[*The sound of the toilet, the sink.* DAD *pokes his head into* MAE'S *room, all squinty-eyed.*]

DAD: Rise and shine!

MAE: Are you serious? What time is it?

DAD: Five-thirty. We gotta hit the road, kid

[MAE *starts to bundle herself up and slowly crosses into the kitchen.* COWBOY *is still with her.*]

MAE: God. I don't think I've been up this early since . . .
    I don't know
    I feel like I'm about to take the SAT or something

DAD: I feel like someone's about to have a baby

    . . .

    Sit down. I want to play you something

[DAD *disappears.* MAE *sits.*]

MAE: Ugh
I'm nervous

COWBOY: You're fine

MAE: I'm not fine. I'm nervous
Ugh. I feel sick to my stomach

COWBOY: You want me to fuck it out of you?

MAE: . . .

COWBOY: I can fuck it out of you, if you want me to fuck it out of you
That feeling. In your stomach
I can fuck you until you don't feel that way anymore
Until you don't feel anything anymore
I can obliterate you, by fucking you, if you want me to

[*Music!* DAD *bounds upstairs. He's smiling. Very pleased with himself. He's carrying some kind of small music-making device. His laptop? His phone? The music comes out small and tinny so that we have to lean in just a bit to hear it.*]

DAD: This is my theme song

MAE: What?

DAD: This is my theme song. For cancer
I decided

MAE: Your theme song?

DAD: When your mom was sick, she had a theme song
She used to play it for me when I drove her to treatments

MAE: You guys were weird

DAD: Some of the lyrics are a little overdramatic but I think it's a pretty good song

[*The song plays. It is incredibly cheesy. But still the kind of song that can make you cry. We're all going to die. And you're not young anymore. And your childhood is gone. And you're full of regret. And your mother is dead. And there's no one to hold you. And you're not dying yet so you have to keep fighting. And it's going to hurt. And the hospital is cold and dark, etc., etc.* MAE *and* DAD *both tear up listening to it. At some point,* DAD *says: "This is my favorite part."*]

MAE: It's a good song

[*He smiles at her.*]

DAD: Alright. You ready? We've got to get across the pass

•◆•

[MAE *and her siblings*—HANNAH, MATTHEW, *and* JENNY—*in a hospital room.* DAD *is sleeping in the bed.* MAE *is knitting. Something bright blue. She's not very good at it.* MATTHEW *is curled up in one of Tiffany's blankets. Down the hallway in an empty lobby is a giant glistening gong.*]

MATTHEW: The Hardy family smell

HANNAH: What about it?

MATTHEW: True or false?

HANNAH: Obviously true

JENNY: It's mothballs

MATTHEW: It's not mothballs

JENNY: I think it's mothballs

MATTHEW: It's not. It's a human smell. You know, like the smell of our skin or something

JENNY: Camille told me that our house smelled like mothballs and chocolate chip cookies

MATTHEW: It does but that's not the Hardy family smell

HANNAH: I used to notice it in Matthew's room after he'd been sleeping

MATTHEW: It's not my fault! I didn't have a window!

HANNAH: Well that's where I noticed it. And then one day I woke up and I smelt the stench of Matthew on my pillow and I thought, "Oh god. It's me too."

MATTHEW: It's not just me. It's all of us. The whole clan. The Hardy family smell

JENNY: Every family has a smell

HANNAH: But I think ours is particularly pungent

JENNY: No

HANNAH: I do! I feel like people have told me on multiple occasions: "Hannah. Your family has a certain smell. Every time I come over to your house, I smell it." If every family had a smell as strong as ours, then why would someone say, "Hannah. Your family has a certain smell"? They wouldn't

MATTHEW: Yeah, they just wouldn't

JENNY: I guess not . . .

MAE: Do you think it bothers our lovers? Do you think they love us / despite our smell?

HANNAH [*under her breath*]: Don't call them your *lovers*

JENNY: EVERYBODY HAS A SMELL

MAE: Despite our *strong* smell

MATTHEW: Maybe they like it

HANNAH: I don't like it. I'm disgusted by it. How can they like it

MATTHEW: I don't know. Maybe they want to stuff their faces into our necks and just sniff us up

HANNAH: I think they *tolerate* it

JENNY: I once dated a guy who smelled really bad to me in the beginning but then by the end—he didn't smell at all!

HANNAH: I think it's an oil gland. I do! We're all really oily

MATTHEW: We are. We are really oily people

HANNAH: And we smell

MATTHEW: *Like what?*

MAE: Musty

HANNAH: Like dank and
    Like mildew

MAE: Musty musty musty

HANNAH: Like something fermenting

MATTHEW: A little like BO

HANNAH: Well that's just BO, probably

MATTHEW: I think our family scent is a little like BO and I'm talking totally independent of literal BO

HANNAH: Okay

JENNY: Dank earth

MATTHEW: Oh come on

JENNY: What? I think we smell a little like wet earth

MATTHEW: Don't romanticize it!

JENNY: Or the ocean

MAE: We do not smell like the ocean   MATTHEW: We do not!

HANNAH: Mold. Mildew. Musty. BO. And egg

MAE: There's something sweet, though

JENNY: Mothballs
    I swear to god there's just a touch of mothballs

MATTHEW: Does it come from Dad or Mom or is it a combo?

HANNAH: Mom

JENNY: Mom

MAE: I think it's gotta be a combo

[HANNAH *sniffs herself.*]

HANNAH: I can't smell it

MAE: That's because you took a shower

[HANNAH *and* MAE *start sniffing themselves, trying to detect the Hardy Family Smell.*]

MATTHEW: You can't smell it on yourself, guys! That's the whole problem. You have to smell it on each other.

[*They start sniffing each other.* JENNY *is not into it.*]

JENNY: Oh you guys. I almost forgot—
    Everyone gets a baseball cap

[JENNY *pulls out four baseball caps.*]

MAE: What?

MATTHEW: Why?

JENNY: This lady I work with told me about it
    She says that at the hospital everyone should wear a baseball cap
    And then if you need to cry
    You pull the cap down over your eyes
    And you can cry in private

MATTHEW: That's / corny

MAE: That's stupid

JENNY: I thought it was really sweet

MATTHEW: If I cry, I'm just going to cry in front of you all and you're
    just gonna have to deal with it

[HANNAH *is still sniffing her siblings, trying to find the smell.*]

HANNAH: Here we go! Here it is! Jenny smells like it!

JENNY: Stop. I was in the car. I haven't showered

MATTHEW: Yup. That's it. That's definitely it.

[DAD *coughs.*]

MAE: Dad?

HANNAH: Dad?

[*They listen—on edge.*]

MAE [*whispering*]: Are you awake?

MATTHEW: I think he's sleeping

MAE: Can you cough when you're asleep?

MATTHEW: Sure. You can cough when you're in a coma

MAE: Really?

HANNAH: He's probably not even sleeping. He's probably just listening with his eyes closed. He's always doing that. Dad? Are you just resting your eyes?

JENNY: Is he going to be able to talk when he wakes up?

MATTHEW: Jesus Christ, Jenny!

JENNY: What? I don't know!

HANNAH: Yeah, he's talking. He was talking this morning. He sounds a little funny, though, just FYI

MATTHEW: It's not like he had a stroke!

JENNY [*on the verge of tears*]: Why are his lips shiny?

HANNAH: I don't know

MAE: The nurses put lip-gloss on him

[JENNY *pulls down her baseball cap and cries.*]

MATTHEW: Oh my god. Do you smell that? Someone has a candy bar

HANNAH: Are you guys hungry? / You wanna eat?

MATTHEW: Oh my god
Chocolate and peanut butter
Oh my god. I'm so hungry
It's like I'm eating it with my nostrils

MAE: Yes, I'm starving

[MATTHEW *eats the air with his nostrils.*]

HANNAH: Okay, well, let's just unpack it on this table

[HANNAH *starts pulling items out of two big brown paper sacks. Avocados, etc.*]

MAE: Jenny? You alright?

JENNY [*still with her baseball cap pulled down*]: Yeah, I'm fine

MATTHEW: Jesus, Hannah! Why did you buy avocados?

HANNAH: I don't know, I was just trying to get things that were filling. And healthy

MATTHEW: Do you even have a knife? This is like the messiest lunch ever

HANNAH: There's a butcher knife JENNY [*from underneath her
wrapped in the dishtowel   baseball cap*]: I love avocados

MATTHEW [*still unpacking*]: Grapefruit, are you / serious?

MAE: We should've ordered Chinese food

HANNAH: Well, I'm / sorry

MATTHEW: It's just. I'm hungry. / I want to eat more than an avocado

MAE: Uh-oh Mattie's hungry

HANNAH: I thought the sandwiches looked terrible. I thought this would be better. Also. Jenny's doctors told her she's not supposed to eat meat or gluten

JENNY: Sorry

MAE AND MATTHEW: Sorry

[*A moment of them all unpacking food, slicing things, etc.*]

HANNAH: So what's it been like at home, Mae?

MATTHEW: Yeah how's he been doing at home?

MAE: Fine, it's been totally fine

HANNAH: How are his symptoms?

MAE: Fine, I think

HANNAH: Does he still have mouth sores?

MAE: I don't know

MATTHEW: Is his mouth still really dry?

MAE: Mattie. I don't ask him

MATTHEW: Well   HANNAH: Is he doing   JENNY: You guys, I think
   why not?   his exercises?   I have to go soon

MAE: I don't know! We don't talk about it!

HANNAH: Is he eating the Amaranth I sent him?

MAE: The what?

HANNAH: I sent him some seeds   JENNY: You guys I think I have
   to grow Amaranth. It's a   to go
   super green. / It's supposed
   to be good for Vitamin C   MATTHEW: Right now?

MAE: Oh yes! He loves it   JENNY: I'm sorry. I have to work
                                      tonight
MATTHEW: You guys Jenny has
   to go

MAE: Oh

JENNY: I have to work tonight. I'm sorry

HANNAH: Don't worry about it, honey

JENNY: But I can drive back tomorrow morning!

MAE: I think he's supposed to be going home today . . .

MATTHEW: He doesn't look like he's going home today

MAE: I know but that's the plan

JENNY: Do you think he's going to wake up soon?

HANNAH: He's just resting

JENNY [*on the verge of tears again*]: Do you think I'm going to get to see him ring the gong?

HANNAH: I don't know, honey. If he wakes up and he feels well enough, we'll make him ring the gong

MAE: Mattie. Stop eating. Serve people

MATTHEW: Sorry

JENNY: I really want a picture with all of us and the gong. When Camille's mom finished treatment her whole PEO group came to see her ring the gong and there were like balloons and everything.

HANNAH: We'll just have to see how it goes

MATTHEW [*still unpacking*]: What the fuck is this cheesecake

HANNAH: It's for Jenny.

MATTHEW: Oh shit. Sorry Jenny

MAE: Stop swearing

JENNY: It's okay

HANNAH: It's a surprise for Jenny.

MAE: Happy Birthday, Jenny!

MATTHEW: It's still frozen

JENNY: I mean, it's not even my birthday for eleven more days, it's okay But thanks Hannah! That's really sweet

HANNAH: You like cheesecake right? I hope that's right

JENNY: I love cheesecake

MAE: I thought you weren't eating dairy?

HANNAH: Oh no! I'm sorry

JENNY: No! It's fine! I
love cheesecake

MAE: Are there / candles?

HANNAH: Mattie! Careful with that knife!

MATTHEW: Look at this avocado you guys
    The whole thing is pit
    There's barely any flesh on it
    It's just a giant pit

JENNY: I like them when the pit is itty-bitty
    You know what I mean?
    You open up the avocado
    And there's just this itty-bitty pit
    It's so cute

HANNAH: Avocados and penises, I'm telling you
    You just never know what you're gonna get

JENNY: Stop

HANNAH: I'm serious—
    You buy the biggest, fleshiest avocado at the store
    And you open it up
    And it has an *itty-bitty* pit
    Or vice versa, or whatever
    Like when I was first with Michael I was like: That's a big man. I
    bet he's going to have, you know, a tiny—

JENNY: Oh my god stop it stop it Hannah

HANNAH: But he had a pretty big one
    I mean, it looks tiny next to his body
    But it's actually pretty big

MAE: I don't like big penises

HANNAH: None of us like big penises

MATTHEW: This conversation is making me uncomfortable

HANNAH: What? I said I *don't* like them
That should make you feel good

MATTHEW: It doesn't make me feel good! Why are you saying that?

HANNAH: I don't mean you specifically
I just mean you as "A Man"
No pressure

MAE: We love your penis, Matthew
We don't / care what it looks like

JENNY: Seriously you guys. Stop

MAE: I am being serious!

JENNY: We shouldn't make fun of men's bodies either. It's terrible

MAE: Yeah, we're sorry for how society oppresses / your body, Mattie

JENNY: I'm serious!
I don't care if you're tall or short or bald or have a weird penis

MATTHEW: I don't have a weird penis / for the record

MAE: All of our children are going to be bald, you guys. Newsflash

JENNY: There's nothing wrong with being bald!

MAE: Tell that to baby Liam

HANNAH: I know. I feel so bad

JENNY: It's not a bad thing to be bald!!!!

HANNAH: It's like. Sorry Liam. Mommy's giving you bad skin, cancer, Alzheimer's, Parkinson's, and Male Pattern Baldness.

MATTHEW: And the Hardy family smell!

HANNAH: And the Hardy family smell!

MAE [*a little too loud*]: I mean
    Don't feel too bad for Liam
    At least he's inheriting Michael's big-ass dick

JENNY: Shh, shh, shhh!

[*They look at* DAD.]

HANNAH: Dad? Are you sleeping?

MAE: See. Whatever. He's sleeping

DAD: Mae?

JENNY: You woke him up!!

DAD: Were you talking to me?

HANNAH: No, Dad. Go back to sleep   MAE: I'm here, Dad

DAD: I want some water. I'm thirsty

JENNY: Can we give him water?

MAE: Hi Dad

HANNAH: Hi Dad

DAD: Why are you all wearing baseball caps?

HANNAH: Shh. Dad. You shouldn't be talking

JENNY: I have one for you too, Dad. If you want one. [*to her siblings*]
    Should I give him one?

HANNAH: In a minute

MAE: Dad, you have to have water off of one of these sponges
    Like Jesus

[MAE *takes a little sponge that is attached to a stick and dunks it in water.*]

Here, Dad—
I'll be the criminal
And you be Jesus
I'm going to give you water on a sponge

MATTHEW: The criminal didn't give him water. The criminal was up there on the cross with him

MAE: Well I'll be the one who gives him water
Are you ready, Dad? Here comes the water. You're Jesus

[DAD *sucks on the sponge.*]

DAD: I want to drink

MAE: I know. But you can't drink

DAD: Will you ask Iris?

JENNY: Hannah already asked Iris, Dad. She says you have to use the sponge

DAD: I just want to drink some water

HANNAH: Here. I can ask her again

[HANNAH *goes to ask Iris.*]

MAE: How are you feeling?

[DAD *smiles.*]

You're all done! You're doing so good

[*They eat.* DAD *sucks his sponge.* MAE *stops eating and picks up her knitting again.*]

JENNY: It's like we're on a picnic

     . . .

    Dad. It's like we're on a picnic
    Hannah bought a cheesecake. It's for me

[*After a moment,* HANNAH *returns.*]

HANNAH: She says, "No drinking"
    But you can keep sucking your sponge
    You want me to dunk it for you again?
    Here. I'll dunk it for you again

[HANNAH *dunks the sponge in water and gives it back to* DAD.]

JENNY: Where'd these blankets come from?

MATTHEW: Here, Hannah. I made you a plate. Eat

MAE: Tiffany

HANNAH: Thanks hon

JENNY: Tiffany?

DAD [*with the sponge in his mouth*]: Tiffany at the office

MAE: She knits

DAD [*still with the sponge in his mouth*]: The apricot one is Mae's. And the teal one is mine

HANNAH: How's the job search going, Mae?

MAE: It's going

HANNAH: Have you started?

MAE: I have a severance. I don't have to start

HANNAH: Mae! You have to start! It's not easy to find a job anymore!

MAE: I'm going to start. After this is over. I'm going to take care of it

JENNY: What kind of cheese is this?

MATTHEW: Tillamook [*pronounced Tilla-muck*]

HANNAH: As long as you start. That's the hardest part.

JENNY: No, what *kind*?

MATTHEW: It's Tillamook cheese

MAE: It's cheddar cheese, Jenny

HANNAH: You know, maybe this is your opportunity. You know what I'm saying?

. . .
. . .
. . .

Mae? To start over. Really think about what you want to do with your life

MATTHEW: It's the best kind of cheddar cheese in Washington state

MAE: Tillamook is in Oregon

MAE: I don't want to think about what I want to do with my life

HANNAH: I mean, you should think about it. Your job sounded pretty awful, to be honest. All that stress. Ugh. Is it really worth it?

MATTHEW: God. Oregon is always beating us at everything.

JENNY: No they aren't!

MATTHEW: Football . . . The deepest lakes . . .

MAE: Hannah

HANNAH: I'm just asking! It's just a question!

MATTHEW: Hannah. Michael's calling

HANNAH: Oh! It's probably Liam

JENNY: Dad! It's the baby!

MAE: Do you want to talk to the baby, Dad?

MATTHEW [*answering* HANNAH's *phone*]: Hi Michael. I'm going to pass you to Hannah

HANNAH [*taking the phone from* MATTHEW]: Hello?

JENNY: Is it him??

HANNAH: Hi Liam. Hi baby
    Are you having fun?

JENNY: What's he saying?

HANNAH: Uh-huh

MAE: Hannah, let Dad talk to him

HANNAH [*to Mae*]: One sec
    . . .
    [*back to the phone*] Oooh are you making cookies?
    . . .
    What kind of cookies?

MAE: Hannah

HANNAH: . . .
    . . .
    . . .
    . . .
    Sugar cookies. That sounds fun
    . . .
    Do you want to talk to your granddad?
    . . .
    . . .
    Here I'm going to hand the phone to your granddad? Okay baby?

[HANNAH *hands off the phone to* DAD.]

DAD: Who is it?

MAE: It's Liam   JENNY: Dad. It's the baby

DAD: Hello

[*A long moment of* DAD *listening to the baby. Everyone is riveted. Maybe* MATTHEW *takes a picture on his phone.*]

[*to* HANNAH] He's not saying anything

HANNAH: You have to talk to him

DAD: What am I supposed to say?

HANNAH: Just talk

DAD: Hi Liam
It's your granddad
How are you doing?

[*He looks at the phone.*]

Are you sure he's on there?

HANNAH [*talking into the phone*]: Hi Liam. Hi baby. Say hi to Granddad

[HANNAH *and* DAD *both listen, glued to the phone. Finally, they hear something.*]

That's him

DAD: That's him?

HANNAH: Yeah that's him. He's talking to you

DAD: What's he saying?

HANNAH: Hi Liam. Can you say hi to Granddad?
Say, "Hi Granddad." "Hi Granddad."

[*They listen.*]

Can you hear him?

DAD: Uh-huh

HANNAH: I think he's tired
Michael? Yeah, I think he's tired
No we're all doing good, yeah. Thanks
[*to her siblings*] Michael says hi

MAE: Hi Michael

MATTHEW: Hi Michael

[HANNAH *steps away from the group.*]

HANNAH [*hushed*]: Hey
Today I think
I don't know
Why don't I call you tonight?
Huh?
I said, why don't I call you tonight
from the hotel?

JENNY: Mae. Is that a scarf?

MAE: No. I'm knitting a
sweater

No, no he's doing good. We're all
doing good but I should probably—

JENNY: Look Dad! Mae is
knitting a sweater

Okay sounds good
Love you

DAD: I know

Bye

MAE: He gave me the yarn

MATTHEW: It's pretty

JENNY: Yarn is so expensive! I knit someone a scarf once and it cost me ninety dollars

MATTHEW: Who's it for?

MAE: Ian

JENNY: You're knitting it for Ian?????   MATTHEW: Are you crazy?!

HANNAH [*rejoining the group*]: What's going on?

JENNY: Mae's knitting a sweater for Ian!!!!!

HANNAH: Mae that's crazy

MAE: It's for his birthday

HANNAH: I thought you guys weren't talking

MAE: I mean, I'm still going to give him something for his birthday

MATTHEW: Mae. That's pretty nuts. You don't want him to think you're obsessed or something

MAE: I'm the one who broke up with him!

MATTHEW: Or pathological!   JENNY: I thought it was mutual

MAE: It's complicated

MATTHEW: That's a little psycho, Mae. I'm not going to lie

HANNAH: Have you heard of the curse?

JENNY: Oooh god! Oh no! / The curse

MAE: What are you talking about?   MATTHEW: The curse?

HANNAH: You knit someone a sweater, they break up with you, unless you've been together five years or longer

MAE: But we're already broken up!!!

JENNY: I can't believe you haven't heard of the curse

MATTHEW: I've never heard of the curse

HANNAH: Well, if you knit him that sweater, you're never getting back together, trust me

MAE: (A) We're not getting back together and (B) that's not a real curse

HANNAH: It is! It is a real curse! It happened to me

MAE: With who?

HANNAH: With Johnny

MAE: You did not break up over a sweater!

HANNAH: No, we did not. But I knit him a sweater. And we broke up. Like three months later

MAE: That doesn't count

HANNAH: We were going to get married!

MAE: You were *not*

JENNY: It's a real curse, Mae. Trust me. It happened to one of my friends, too. Their relationship was going great. Really cute relationship. And then boom. She knit him a sweater and he was gone.

MATTHEW: Huh

HANNAH: And also. Like two years after Johnny and I broke up. He got this horrible, rare blood cancer. And he died.

MAE: What?!

JENNY: I didn't know Johnny died!!

HANNAH: And the way I found out is that one day I got this package in the mail. From his mother. And I opened it up. And it was the sweater. She thought I'd want to keep it, or something. So yeah. There's definitely a curse.

JENNY: Hannah! I can't believe you didn't tell us that Johnny died!

HANNAH: Yeah. I didn't tell anyone. I'm sorry. I didn't want to talk about it.

JENNY: That's terrible. You should have told me. He was someone I knew. For like a long time.

HANNAH: I just didn't want to talk about it. I'm sorry

JENNY: Dad? Did you know that Johnny died?

DAD: I think I did know that

HANNAH: No you didn't, Dad. I didn't tell anyone but Michael. I'm sorry.

MATTHEW: It's okay, Hannah

HANNAH: I mean, it's probably not. Okay. But thanks

[*They sit for a minute.*]

It's weird when someone you hate dies of cancer.
I'm pretty sure I wished that he'd die of cancer. Like verbally wished that he'd die of cancer. More than once. Maybe several times. I'm pretty sure that I said he was fundamentally a force for evil. I'm pretty sure I said that if he died the world would get a net gain in goodness and purity and kindness and love.
But yeah. I didn't mean it. I don't think I meant it. Maybe I meant it? I guess I did mean it. At the time. In any case. I'm sorry he died. I didn't want him to actually die. But anyway.

MATTHEW: The sweater didn't kill him

HANNAH: No
Maybe?

[HANNAH *pulls her baseball cap down.*]

MATTHEW: It didn't

HANNAH: But it's not just me.
   It's everyone.
   There is a curse.
   You knit someone a sweater and they break up with you.

MAE: Or die of cancer

HANNAH: Yeah

MAE: Well I'm not worried about it

[MAE *fingers her lump.*]

JENNY: I can't believe that happened to him. Poor Johnny. I never
   would've thought that *that* was going to happen to him

DAD: Last time I was here, I met this very nice man from Philadelphia
   who was here with his daughter. She's an old daughter. In her
   fifties. And the man is old too. Maybe eighty-two

MAE: Uh-huh

DAD: He has cancer. And it's terminal. There's nothing they can do

MATTHEW: Why did they come all the way to Seattle from Philadelphia if it's terminal cancer?

DAD: I don't know. To extend his life? I don't know
   They're a black family

JENNY: Dad, you don't have to comment on their race

DAD: What? It's true?

JENNY: But if they were a white family you wouldn't have said
   anything

DAD: It's a detail. / It's a detail of my story

HANNAH: Should he be talking?

DAD: I can talk! I can talk as long as I talk carefully

HANNAH: I thought she said you shouldn't be talking

DAD: I just want to tell this one story

HANNAH: Well if you tear your throat up . . .

MATTHEW: It's fine

[DAD *clears his throat.*]

DAD: This is just to show you

[*He clears his throat.*]

    The sort of people we have here

[*He clears his throat.*]

    The sort of community and—
    You know, I'm really very lucky

MAE: We know

DAD: I mean it
     . . .
    So this man from Philadelphia—

JENNY [*under her breath*]: A black man

MATTHEW: Shut up, Jenny

DAD: —was here and I met him. And we became sort of friends. Or friendly. And they had to drill four holes in his head and put beads in his skull and then shoot the radiation through the beads at his brain

MATTHEW: Jesus

DAD: It's called a neutron machine. It's called neutron therapy
They only have three of these machines
In the world

[*counting on his fingers*]

Tokyo, Houston, and here
So
Again, just to show you how lucky
And the sort of things we're dealing with here
. . .
I mean, it really is amazing

JENNY: It is amazing
It is an amazing place

DAD: So he's here to have
These beads put in his forehead
And then they're going to send him home to Philadelphia. To live. With these beads in his forehead. And they're just the nicest people. His whole family. Anyway, one day in recovery, I was in the lounge making my yogurt with sardines

JENNY: Dad. Ew

DAD: It goes down

JENNY: Just ew

DAD: And this woman—the daughter—she was looking out the window. Not making eye contact, or anything like that. And her shoulders were just shaking. Up and down and up and down. And I thought. My god. She's crying. I've got to do something

MAE: Oh no, Dad. What did you do?

DAD: No wait this is a good story

MAE: You should just ignore people when they're crying. You shouldn't bother them

DAD: Well I went up behind her

MAE: Oh god

DAD: And I gave her a hug from behind

MAE: Oh god   JENNY: Dad!   MATTHEW [*laughing*]: I love this story

DAD: And she just about jumped out of her skin

JENNY: What did she say?

DAD: And it turns out—she wasn't crying

JENNY: What did she say?

DAD: And I said: "I'm sorry. I just wanted to give you a hug. I thought you were crying."
And she said: "No I'm not crying. I'm sick. I'm sick, too. And it makes my shoulders shake."
And then we laughed.
I think she liked it.
I think she was touched.
I think she got a little bit teary-eyed, if you want to know the truth.
. . .
So
That's the kind of place this is
. . .
. . .

HANNAH: Why are we being all sad? We should be happy!

DAD: I'm not sad

HANNAH: We should be celebrating! This is a happy day!

DAD: You guys should go out and go shopping. Enjoy each other's company. / You don't need to be stuck in here with me

JENNY: We're not going to go shopping

HANNAH: You know what we need to have sometime soon? A family dance party

JENNY: A family dance party?

HANNAH: Yeah someone needs to get married so we can have another family dance party

MATTHEW: Not it!

MAE: Not it!   JENNY: Not it!

DAD: Well not me either!

MATTHEW: Jenny's got a girlfriend

JENNY: Yeah but I'm not going to marry her!

HANNAH: Well it's gotta be one of you. I did my duty

JENNY: Dad I have to go soon. Do you think we could ring the gong?

HANNAH: Jenny, honey, I think we should wait / until he's feeling better

DAD: We can ring the gong

JENNY [*exiting to the lobby*]: I'm going to go ask Iris / if we can ring the gong

HANNAH: Mattie. Get off your phone

MAE: He's texting his girlfriend

MATTHEW: I'm not texting my girlfriend

HANNAH: I didn't know you had a girlfriend!!

MATTHEW: I don't have a girlfriend. JUST LET ME TEXT

MAE: Haha remember when Mom was in the hospital and Mattie brought Ashley

HANNAH: Oh my god / you were all over her

MATTHEW: Mom loved Ashley

MAE: Mom thought Ashley was "alright"

HANNAH: Mom had crushes on all my ex-boyfriends

MATTHEW [*still fiddling with his phone*]: Your ex-boyfriends were assholes

HANNAH: Well maybe Mom was into assholes

MAE: Dad? Were you an asshole?

MATTHEW [*into the phone as he exits*]: Hello?

DAD: What?

HANNAH: Were you a good boy or a bad boy?

MAE: I bet all the ladies loved you, huh?

DAD: I don't know. You'd have to ask them

JENNY [*in the doorway*]: I can't find Iris. Can you come / help me?

DAD [*with his eyes closed*]: Your mother loved me

HANNAH: Here, I'm coming

[HANNAH *follows* JENNY *into the lobby.* MAE *alone with* DAD.]

MAE: Dad?

    . . .

    Are you asleep?

[MAE *looks at her* DAD. *He's sleeping. She quietly picks up the forgotten picnic—placing napkins and paper plates into the brown paper bags. A* NURSE *enters. He looks like an ordinary nurse at first, but then something shimmers, and he becomes* COWBOY . . .]

NURSE: Hey there

MAE [*startled*]: Hi

[MAE *scurries out of the room, taking the garbage with her.* NURSE *exits as* MATTHEW *enters.*]

MATTHEW [*to* NURSE]: Excuse me

[DAD *opens his eyes. In the background, through the hospital room window, we can see* MAE *having a private mini-breakdown.*]

Hey. Sorry. [*Indicating the phone*] Stupid work stuff
. . .
How're you doing?

DAD: Alright.
Could I have some water?

[MATTHEW *hesitates for a second and then pours* DAD *a glass of water. He hands* DAD *the cup.*]

Thank you.

MATTHEW: No problem.

[DAD *drinks. Eventually,* JENNY *returns, and* DAD *hands the cup back to* MATTHEW. *In the background, we can still see* MAE *melting down.*]

JENNY: I still can't find Iris. The lobby's empty

MATTHEW: Where's Hannah?

JENNY: I don't know. I lost her. What am I supposed to do about Iris?!

MATTHEW: I'm sure she'll be back in five minutes

JENNY: But I have to go

MATTHEW: What do you want me to say, Jenny? DAD: What's the problem?

JENNY: I want to be here when you ring the gong but Iris is missing and I have to go

DAD: Well why don't we just do it real quick and then we'll do it again for real when Iris is back

JENNY: You're sure you're feeling well enough? MATTHEW: I think it's against the rules to ring the gong without Iris . . .

DAD: Yeah, I'm feeling great. I just need to sit up

[*He sits himself up and climbs out of bed with some difficulty. It's a little terrifying to see him standing upright.* HANNAH *enters.*]

HANNAH: Whoa, Dad. What's going on?

MATTHEW: Apparently we're going to ring the gong without Iris . . .

JENNY: Do you want my arm, Dad?

DAD: I'm fine. I'm just taking it slowly

JENNY: Hold on, just let me get some snacks / for the road

HANNAH: Where's Mae?

JENNY: I don't know we lost her

HANNAH: Should we wait for her?

JENNY: I have to go!

[DAD *walks slowly and carefully through the door, down a little hallway, and into the lobby.*]

MATTHEW [*to his siblings*]: Are you sure this is okay?

HANNAH: Hold on. Let me get my camera

JENNY: Dad! Wait! He's going—

HANNAH: Well go after him!

JENNY [*exiting*]: Dad!

HANNAH [*under her breath*]: Where the fuck is my camera???

MATTHEW [*to* HANNAH]: I just feel like we're gonna jinx it

HANNAH: Jinx what?

MATTHEW: By ringing the gong. It's like: "Woohoo! All cured!"

HANNAH: Mattie, that's morbid!

[MAE *re-enters from the hallway, a little teary-eyed.*]

MAE: Hey. Sorry. What's happening?

HANNAH: We're just gonna take a picture in front of the gong so Jenny can go

MAE: Is that okay with Iris?

MATTHEW: I don't know. I think she's gonna be pissed . . .

HANNAH [*exiting*]: Come on, guys. Chop chop

MAE: You okay, Mattie?

MATTHEW: I wasn't texting my girlfriend

MAE: I know

MATTHEW: No one texts me

MAE: I know. I'm sorry.
   No one texts me either

MATTHEW: Are *you* okay?

JENNY [*calling from the lobby*]: Are you guys coming?????

MATTHEW [*calling back*]: Sorry!

JENNY: Oh my god, I'm going to be *so late*

[MATTHEW *exits down the hallway.* MAE *lingers for just a moment, overwhelmed. As she exits, she pulls down her baseball cap.*]

HANNAH: Okay, I've got my camera!

JENNY: Isn't there supposed to be a little ceremony or something

HANNAH: I don't know, honey. I think you just ring it

DAD: Should I ring it?

MATTHEW: Just fake ring it, Dad

DAD: I'm not going to fake ring it

MATTHEW: Just pose for the picture with Jenny and then you can ring it for real when Iris gets back

HANNAH: Come on, Jenny. Go stand by Dad

JENNY: Aren't you all going to be in the picture?

HANNAH: Mattie, Mae. Get in the picture

JENNY: Is anyone going to say anything?

HANNAH: Mattie. Read the inscription

MATTHEW: Out loud?

HANNAH: Come on, / just read it

MAE: Ring this bell
    Three times well,
    Its toll to—

MAE AND MATTHEW: —clearly say,
    My treatment's done,
    This course is run,
    And I am on my way!

HANNAH: Amen

JENNY: Are you ready, Dad?

DAD: Okay. Here I go   MATTHEW: Just fake ring it, Dad

[DAD *rings the gong. It makes the tiniest, muffliest of sounds.*]

JENNY: Dad that was pathetic

DAD: I thought it was a real gong, one of those kind that reverberates,
    / you know, you barely touch it and it reverberates

MATTHEW: No, it's just a cheap gong

JENNY: It *is* a real gong. It is. You just have to ring it the right way.
    Try it again

DAD: Okay. I'm going to ring it again. I'm going to ring it really loud
    this time

MATTHEW: Not too loud!   JENNY: Ring it, Dad!

MAE: Hannah? You've got the camera?

HANNAH: I've got the camera. I'm filming this whole / thing

DAD: Okay I'm gonna ring it

HANNAH: Okay here goes! We're watching!

JENNY: You're done! You're done! You're done!

[DAD *rings the gong. Once, twice, three times. Four times. Five times. Six times. Seven. It is really loud. It reverberates throughout the hospital.* JENNY *covers her ears.*]

•◆•

[*Back home.* DAD *and* MAE *winterize the garden. The pepper plants are dead.* MAE *breaks the stalks and stuffs them into a big black garbage bag.* DAD *watches. They wear heavy-duty winter coats. It's cold.*]

DAD: So I'm going to ask you those bad questions now

MAE: Okay

DAD: Is that okay?

MAE: It's totally fine

DAD: So what's your plan to support yourself?

MAE: Support myself?

DAD: How are you going to pay your bills?
    And what about health insurance?

MAE: Um . . .

DAD: Are you applying for jobs or—

MAE: Actually I just got an interview

DAD: You did?

MAE: Yeah I was going to tell you about it once I knew how it went

DAD: What kind of interview?

MAE: It's at this boutique firm
    They do sports law

DAD: Do you do sports law?

[*She shrugs.*]

MAE: I've done some entertainment stuff

DAD: That's great! When's the interview?

MAE: This afternoon

DAD: This afternoon! Mae! Are you prepared?

MAE: I'm going to Skype it

DAD: Is that okay?

MAE: Yeah they said it's fine. I told them I was in Washington state

DAD: Did you tell them why?

MAE: No. I just said that I was in Washington state

DAD: Mae! You should tell them why!

MAE: I'm not going to tell them why!

DAD: You don't have to make a big deal of it. Just say you're home
taking care of your dad

MAE: Dad. I'm not going to say that

DAD: Let me give you some advice—
When you're dealing with something like this
It's always best to bring it up early and casually

MAE: Dad. You're stressing me out

DAD: Just hear me out! You want to mention it right away, just
off-the-cuff: *Hey! Thanks for the interview! I'm in Washington
state taking care of my dad but I'd be happy to do something over
Skype.* You never know. Maybe they'll even want you more if
they know why you're away

MAE: Dad. Stop

DAD: What? It's admirable! I'd want to hire a candidate who went home to take care of her dad!
Did you tell them why you lost your job?

MAE: Dad! No!

DAD: You have to tell them why you lost your job! You don't want them to think you were fired. It wasn't your fault!

MAE: I'm going to explain it in person

DAD: On Skype???

MAE: In person on Skype

DAD: Well at least tell them why you're in Washington state

MAE: I already set up the interview. I already didn't mention it. There's nothing I can do. You're just stressing me out by telling me what I did wrong

DAD: What if they think you're on some kind of pleasure cruise?

MAE: They don't think I'm on a pleasure cruise!

DAD: What if they think you should've flown back for the interview?

MAE: The lady said Skype was fine. I asked her if I should fly back and she said, "No."

DAD: Let me tell you a story—

MAE: Dad—

DAD: Just—
Give me, okay—
I'm going to tell you a story to illustrate my point

MAE: I don't want a story. I'm just going to do the interview and see how it goes—

DAD: Just let me tell you a story—

MAE: Okay, fine.

DAD: The other week . . .
   I was really stressing out about some shipments that hadn't
   come in

MAE: Uh-huh

DAD: And this woman—one of our vendors—was really giving me
   the runaround, you know, follow up in a few days and bullshit
   like that. And I finally said to her: "You know, lady. I'm sorry but
   I'm actually away from the office undergoing cancer treatments
   right now, and it's *really* hard for me to follow up." And wouldn't
   you know it was all taken care of within twenty-four hours. Like
   that.

[DAD *really thinks this is a profound story. His voice wavers.*]

   So. You see
   Sometimes you just have to tell people what's going on
   And they'll take care of you

MAE: Yeah but that's not the same thing at all

DAD: Okay Mae

MAE: It's not! She was giving you the runaround. She owed something to *you*. And you were just saying don't give me a hard time
   right now. But I *want something* from these people. I want them
   to *give me something* that they don't owe me so it's just weird,
   frankly, to bring up your cancer

DAD: Okay Mae whatever you—

MAE: What?

DAD: Okay—

MAE: What?! It is! It's weird to bring it up! "My dad has cancer. Give me a job." It's weird.

DAD: I was just trying to explain why sometimes it doesn't hurt to—

MAE: But it's not the same thing!

DAD: It *is* the same thing!

MAE: No it's not! It's two entirely different situations! It's not the same thing at all!

DAD: Okay I think we're done

MAE: What?

DAD: We're done
The conversation is done

MAE: Don't walk away from me!

DAD: Sorry I'm not walking away from you

MAE: Do you understand why you're wrong?

DAD: We're done, Mae

MAE: But you're wrong

DAD: Okay	MAE: I'm just trying to explain to you why
Okay	you're wrong! You're wrong! Argh!
We're done, Mae	Why are you so *stupid* sometimes? It's
We're done	obvious you're wrong!

[DAD *goes back inside.* MAE *alone in the garden. Maybe she catches a glimpse of* COWBOY. *She watches him for a moment and then he's gone.*]

•◆•

[MAE's *bedroom at night. It's dark. A face appears in* MAE's *window. She opens the window.*]

MAE: Hi

MAC: Hi

MAE: Thanks for coming

MAC: Of course

MAE: You wanna come in?

MAC: Heh heh
     This is really great

[MAC *hauls himself up onto the windowsill.*]

     Should I just—

MAE: Shhh. We have to be quiet

MAC: Oh fuck. Is your dad here?

MAE: Yeah. He's sleeping

MAC: So this is like your childhood bedroom?

MAE: Actually, it's Hannah's room

MAC: Weird!

[MAC *is still sitting on the windowsill, his feet dangling above* MAE's *bed.*]

     Um
     I'm going to have to stand on the bed for a second to get inside
     the room

MAE: That's okay

MAC: Do you want me to take my shoes off first?

MAE: No it's fine

[MAC *puts his feet on the bed and lowers himself down into a squat. They're both sort of squatting on the bed. They don't touch.*]

So here I am
On Hannah's bed

MAE: Yes

[MAC *and* MAE *squat on* HANNAH's *bed.*]

MAC: Do you want to get under the covers?

MAE: In a minute

[MAE *crawls over to* MAC. *She puts her arms around his neck.*]

Is this okay?

MAC: Of course

[*She wraps her legs around his waist. She holds him.*]

MAE: Oh my god
I haven't been touched in so long

[*She holds him.*]

This feels so good, Mac

MAC: I'm glad

MAE: It feels really good. I could do this all night

MAC: I want to make you feel good

MAE: Thanks

[MAE *holds* MAC. *She breathes him in.*]

Wait. Have you been drinking?

MAC: A little

MAE: How drunk are you?

MAC: Not that drunk

MAE: How drunk?

MAC: Just a few beers

MAE: . . .

   . . .

   . . .

   . . .

I wish you hadn't been drinking

MAC: I'm sorry

MAE: It's just, I can smell it, you know

MAC: Sorry Mae

MAE: It's alright

[MAE *stays there—her arms and legs still wrapped around* MAC. *He tries to kiss her but she holds him tight and there's no way to get to her mouth.*]

Can you squeeze me?

MAC: What?

MAE: Just like hold me really tight

[MAC *squeezes* MAE *really tight.*]

Yeah, just squeeze me
As hard as you can

[MAC *squeezes* MAE.]

Yeah

[MAC *squeezes* MAE.]

Don't stop squeezing

[MAC *squeezes* MAE *tight. He releases her.*]

MAC: I'm sorry
My arms are tired

MAE: That's okay

[MAE *and* MAC *sit on* HANNAH's *bed.*]

MAC: Do you still have your rash?

MAE: It's mostly gone

MAC: Can I see it?

[*Knock at the door.* MAE *and* MAC *are petrified.*]

DAD: Mae? Are you in there?
Mae? You asleep?
Can I come in?

. . .

. . .

I'm sorry about earlier
I just don't want you to get in your own way
You inherited that from me, I think

. . .

. . .

Mae?
You sleeping?

. . .

. . .

. . .

I can't sleep

. . .

. . .

. . .

[*Long agonized silence. Finally,* DAD *is gone.*]

MAC: *That was so intense!*

MAE: Maybe you should go

MAC: No, no, no. I'll be quiet
I feel like I'm in high school
I'm so turned on

MAE: Mac? I think I should go talk to him. I think you should go

MAC: No come here. Just kiss me for a minute and then I'll go, I
promise

MAE: Um

MAC: Is that alright?
If I kiss you?

[MAC *pulls* MAE *toward him and kisses her. They make out a little. Then* MAC *pulls away from her.*]

Okay. That's it. You're cut off. Go talk to your dad.

[MAE *laughs. She closes her eyes.*]

MAE: He's probably sleeping

MAC: I don't know

MAE: Don't you think he's asleep?

> . . .
>
> . . .
>
> . . .

[*They stay like that for a minute.* MAE *with her eyes closed.* MAC *holding her at a distance. Then she leans in and kisses him. It's a little sexy, pretty sloppy. Hands under clothes, etc.*]

MAC: You know, I've been thinking about you

MAE: Really?

MAC: Yeah, I've been thinking about you because—
   Wait. How old's your dad?

MAE: Sixty-two

MAC: Yeah, I've been thinking about you because—
   My mom, when she had me, was just nineteen

MAE: Wow

MAC: Yeah
   And when kids used to make fun of me at school and stuff and be mean to me, I used to say: If everyone lives to one-hundred. And my mom is twenty-six and *your* mom is forty-four or whatever.

Then that means that I get eighteen more years with my mom
than you do

MAE [*laughing*]: Oh man that's brutal

MAC: But I mean, of course, that's not true. Because my mom could
die before your dad, I mean, still. Even with everything. It's
possible.

MAE: . . .

MAC: Like my mom lives in California
And I see her like
Once, maybe twice a year if I'm lucky
For a few days at a time
And you've been here for what? Six weeks?
So that's like six *years*
In my book
And even if I added up all the days
All the days I'm going to spend with my mom for the rest of my life
So let's say one week a year times fifty more years that's like
fifty weeks that's like one more year of life, one more year of
actual days, spent together, in each other's company, I mean, after
eighteen years of growing up together, *one more year of days,*
and I know there's like the Internet and phone calls and stuff, but
one more year of *actual days together* in each other's company
before—

MAE: Hey Mac? Can you stop?

MAC: Oh. I'm sorry

MAE: No, no. It's fine. It's just—
This is kind of making me really sad

MAC: I'm sorry, Mae
I just wanted to like—
Talk to you, you know?

I just wanted you to feel like you could talk to me about stuff
I mean, if you needed someone to talk to

MAE: No. I appreciate it

[*She goes to kiss him again, a little more aggressive this time.*]

MAC: Um
   Before I forget
   I don't have a condom

MAE: Oh

MAC: I meant to pick some up on the way but I forgot

MAE: That's okay

MAC: Are you on—

MAE: No. Not right now. I stopped taking it

MAC: Oh. Okay, cool so—

MAE: Wait. Actually. I might have a condom

[MAE *dives over the side of the bed.*]

MAC: I mean, we could also just—
   I mean, I'm probably not even going to cum tonight, if I'm honest

MAE: Hannah used to keep a condom down here
   For
   I don't know
   She was not having sex in high school

MAC: Yeah, me either

MAE: Anyway, someone gave her a condom. And she hid it down here
   Where is it?

Shoot
My mom must've found it and thrown it away

[MAE *still dangling off the side of the bed.* MAC *slaps her ass.*]

Thanks

[MAE *still hanging off the edge of the bed.*]

MAC: Mae? Are you going to come back?

MAE: I'm feeling shy

MAC: That's alright

[MAE *still hanging off the edge of the bed.*]

I used to have this girlfriend who liked it when I poured boiling
water on her boobs

MAE: Really?

MAC: Not boiling
But like kettle water
Almost boiling
On her boobs

MAE: I've never done that

MAC: I used to like . . . give her baths

[MAE *still hanging off the edge of the bed.*]

Hey Mae
We don't have to have sex
If you don't want to do it without a condom

That's totally fine
We can just. Hang out

MAE: I'm just

MAC: Or *cuddle*? I'm down for whatever

MAE: I'm just feeling a little paranoid right now

MAC: That's okay

MAE: Which is stupid

MAC: It's not stupid

MAE: I feel like every blowjob I give is one blowjob closer to death, you know what I'm saying?

MAC: Not really

MAE: Like in terms of time, sure
But also in terms of
Disease
Like when someone's dick is down my throat
All I can think about is
Like
Cancer
And how I'm going to be sixty-two and die
From giving too many blowjobs in my youth
Which won't happen
But I mean, it could
It could actually happen
And I know I shouldn't worry about that
I should just be focusing on my dad
I mean, it's a little selfish to worry about that
It's totally selfish
Because I'm healthy
But I mean, let's be honest

Who knows what the fuck is going on inside of me
I'm breaking out in rashes. I can't sleep. I can't eat
I've had a headache for like the last two weeks
It's like I can feel my body already dying or
Like somehow I skipped that part where you're just grown up and
healthy
And I'm already sick and old
Or I don't know what I'm saying. Mac?
Just fuck me
Just promise you won't cum inside me it's fine
I trust you
  . . .
Mac?

MAC: What?

MAE: What?

MAC: Sorry

MAE: I said, let's have sex

MAC: Sex?

MAE: Yeah
  If you want

MAC: Honestly
  I'm pretty tired
  Right now

MAE: Are you sleeping?

MAC: A little
  Maybe I just fell asleep for a little bit
  I don't know

[MAE *sits up.*]

MAE: Whoa
    All the blood is rushing to my head
    Mac?

[*He's sleeping.*]

    Mac?
    You can't sleep here

[*She pokes him.*]

    Come on, Mac
    Fuck.
    Mac. I have to go check on my dad.

[*She starts to say his name, very patiently, very quietly. A little scared to wake him up.*]

    Mac?
    Mac?
    Mac?
     . . .
     . . .
    Mac?

[*She hits him hard.*]

MAC: Jesus Christ!

MAE: Sorry. You were sleeping

MAC: What time is it?

MAE: You need to go home

MAC: The window is open

MAE: I know

MAC: Was I sleeping?

MAE: Yeah

MAC: God I'm tired
. . .
My shoes are on . . .

MAE: Yeah I know. You need to go

MAC: Sorry. I'm going to sit up

[MAC *sits up. He gathers his things and clambers onto the windowsill.*]

Hey Mae. I'm sorry

MAE: It's alright

MAC: We should do this again sometime when I'm not so tired.
Maybe when it's not so late. Maybe even sometime when it's
light outside . . .

MAE: Sounds good

[*He clambers out the window.*]

MAC: God it's cold out here

[*His face framed in the window . . .*]

You're fucking sexy, do you know that?

MAE: Goodnight

MAC: Goodnight

[MAC *runs off into the night.* MAE *shuts the window and makes a beeline for the door. She opens it.* COWBOY *is framed in the doorway, blocking her exit.*]

COWBOY: Where are you going?

MAE: I need to go check on my dad

COWBOY: You weren't too worried about him before

MAE: No he needs me, he can't / sleep

COWBOY: I'm sure he's sleeping by now

MAE [*fighting to get around him*]: Get the fuck out of my way

COWBOY: SETTLE DOWN

[*She does.*]

MAE: I don't feel good

COWBOY: You know what I do when an animal is sick?

MAE: . . .

COWBOY: I take it out back and I shoot it
It's the merciful thing to do

[MAE *tries to get away from him but he goes after her, grabs her, holds on to her. She collapses into him, exhausted.*]

MAE: Luke? I need you to make love to me slowly and gently and heal my body

COWBOY: I can't do that, Mae

MAE: . . .
      . . .

. . .

. . .

. . .

Obliterate me then

[*He slams her into the wall and fucks her. And maybe at some point . . . * COWBOY *disappears, and we see* MAE *furiously and joylessly masturbating, until her body shudders, and she cums—racked with sobs. Nothing more than empty, grief-ridden release.*]

• ◆ •

[*The bright light of morning. It's snowing.* MAE *emerges bleary-eyed and hungover from the night before.* DAD *is at the table with a special breakfast.*]

MAE: It's snowing!

DAD: I know

MAE: It's all white

DAD: I had to shovel the driveway

MAE: Champagne! Why is there champagne?

DAD: I don't know. I thought we deserved it.

MAE: Are you having some?

DAD: I'm drinking water

MAE: You found the cheesecake!

DAD: It was in the freezer

MAE: It's Jenny's cheesecake

DAD: Why does Jenny have a cheesecake?

MAE: Hannah bought it for her birthday. We forgot to eat it at the hospital

DAD: It's Jenny's birthday!

MAE: I know

DAD: Yesterday! We have to call her!

MAE: She called while you were napping. I told her we'd call her back today

DAD: Don't let me forget

MAE: I won't

[DAD *hands* MAE *a glass of champagne. She takes it. They stand there with their glasses.*]

I rescheduled my interview

DAD: Oh. Is that okay?

MAE: It was no big deal

DAD: Okay . . .

MAE: So I think I should probably fly back for it

DAD: I think so, too

MAE: So I guess I should probably fly back pretty soon

DAD [*gently*]: I think that's good

MAE: So I guess I have to find a place to live

DAD: You will, Mae
I'll miss you
But I think that's good
. . .
For both of us

MAE [*laughing*]: Dad!

DAD: In a nice way!
    You know
    In a nice way

[*They smile at each other. This is all a little painful.*]

MAE: Well cheers

DAD: Cheers

[*She goes to clink glasses. He stops her, explaining . . .*]

    Water

[MAE *drinks her champagne.* DAD *holds his glass.*]

    It's strange but . . .
    In some ways
    This has been one of the most wonderful years of my life

MAE: . . .

DAD: I know. I'm not the same.
    But there are other things. I've gained, so.
      . . .
    Human. Experience.

MAE: . . .

DAD: I'm looking forward, is what I'm—

MAE: That's good

[MAE *drinks her champagne.* DAD *cuts the cake.*]

    We never had a fire!

DAD: No! We didn't

MAE: How's your throat?

DAD: You know. It's fine.

MAE [*meaning the cheesecake*]: Are you having some?

DAD: I'll try a little piece

MAE: Geez. The last time I had cake for breakfast was . . .

DAD: Wait. Do we have candles?

MAE: I can get some

DAD: Why don't you get some candles. We'll sing to Jenny.

[MAE *disappears into the kitchen.* DAD *touches his neck, gingerly. After a moment,* MAE *comes back. She's carrying two tall red dinner candles.*]

MAE: Okay. We're using these

[*She sticks the two candles in the cake.*]

DAD: It looks like the devil
    A devil cake

MAE: It's not a devil cake. It's a cheesecake

DAD: Here let me light them

[DAD *lights the candles. He launches into song.*]

Why was she born so beautiful?
Why was she born at all?
She's no bloomin' use to anyone.
She's no bloomin' use at all.

MAE: What in the world is that?

[DAD *laughs.*]

DAD: It's the Hardy Family Birthday song!

MAE: It is not!!!!!!

DAD: It was when I was a kid! Your Great Uncle Julius used to sing it

MAE: That's a terrible song

DAD: I know

MAE: Sing it again

DAD: *Why was she born so—*

MAE: Wait. Let me get my camera

[MAE *grabs her phone.*]

> Okay, ready?
> Jenny's going to hate this
> Sing it again

DAD: *Why was she born so beautiful?*
Why was she born at all?
She's no bloomin' use to anyone.
She's no—

MAE: Oh shit. One more time
I didn't press it
I'm sorry
[*into the camera*] Hi Jenny

DAD: *Why was she born so beautiful?*
Why was she born at all?
She's no bloomin' use to anyone.

She's no bloomin' use at all.

. . .

Can I blow?

MAE: Yeah, go

[DAD *blows out the candles.* MAE *plays the video back on the phone. We hear* DAD *singing through the phone's speakers—his voice small and far away. They both watch the video.*]

Perfect.

[DAD *tries to eat his cake, but it's difficult to chew, difficult to swallow . . . He makes the best of it.* MAE *watches* DAD *struggling. She fingers her neck. She doesn't touch her cake.*]

DAD: You sleep okay?

MAE: Fine

DAD: I remember when you kids were little and you had nightmares you used to sit outside our door and call for your mother. Just: Mom . . . Mom . . . Mom . . . Over and over again until she finally heard you and got up

MAE: . . .

DAD: I don't know how she heard you. You were so quiet. I never heard you.

[MAE *pushes her cake aside.*]

MAE: Dad? Can I ask you a favor?

DAD: Sure, Mae

MAE: Can you touch the lump in my neck?

DAD: Uh, sure. If you want me to

MAE: I'm sorry. But will you just touch it and tell me if it feels weird?
    I know I'm being stupid. I just—

DAD: No, I can touch it

MAE: Thank you

DAD: Where is it?

MAE: Tucked up behind my jaw bone on the right hand side

[DAD *gently searches for* MAE's *lump under her jawbone.*]

DAD: I can't find it

MAE: It's way up in there

DAD: Sorry. I can't find it

[MAE *takes* DAD's *hand and guides it to her lump.*]

    Oh! Oh! There it is.

[DAD *fingers* MAE's *neck.*]

MAE: What are you doing?

DAD: Just feeling it

[*He considers it carefully. This can take some time.*]

    I think it's fine
    Yeah. It's fine

[*He smiles at her. The whole thing has been a kind of benediction.*]

It's totally fine.

MAE: Thanks

[*Something moves outside the window.*]

DAD: Oh my—

MAE: What? What?

DAD: Shhh. Deer

MAE: Deer?

DAD: Deer!

MAE: Where?

DAD: Right there

MAE: Where?

DAD: Right there, Mae

MAE: I don't see them!
    [*seeing them*] Oh my god!
    Deer! Deer!

DAD: Deer!

MAE: Deer!

[*They both stand for a moment—very still, very quiet—looking out at the deer.*]

DAD: Oh, they're gone.

[*The stage flashes white. Everything white. Feet and feet of snow everywhere. Very bright sun. MAE in the middle of all that white. It hurts our eyes, it's so bright.*]

MAE: And I'm out walking
Further than I've walked in months
And the whole world is cold and white
But the cold feels kind of good on my face
And I feel warm in my coat
And I keep walking
All the way from my apartment to downtown Minneapolis
Until my feet get cold and wet with sweat
And I duck into a Trailblazer looking for some boots.
All the snow boots in all the world are sold out online
I'm not joking. This is not a joke
They are actually sold out
Because people are freaking out
About the Polar Vortex
So I'm not particularly hopeful when I duck into this Trailblazer
But there's a man there holding a box of insoles and he says they have one pair left. Sorels
"What size are you?"
I'm a size seven
"Shoot. These are sixes."
But I try them on anyway . . .
And they fit!
Sorels run big, I tell him. (His name is Eric)
"They're not making any more this season," Eric says
That's crazy! They're all sold out!
"You better be careful walking home. People are going to try to steal those boots from you."
And Eric calls me "the luckiest girl in all of Minneapolis."
And I walk home hugging those boots to my chest.
In the elevator of my building
An old lady is talking to the doorman
He shouts at her, "Pea soup is better! I want pea soup!"
"Sure thing, Bob. I've just gotta get some—"
(The elevator closes)

"—hambone."

She turns to me, explaining: "I've known Bob for twenty-five years. We make things for each other. It's cool."

It *is* cool

"That's what friends are for!"

And I go into my apartment

And I put on my boots

And I think about what I want to eat for dinner

And I start to feel something

That I haven't felt in a while

In a long while

What is this feeling?

Happiness

For no reason at all

Just happiness

Just standing in my living room wearing boots

Just full

Of happiness

For no reason

Just standing in my boots

All alone

[*A phone ringing.* DAD, *very far away. A great distance between them.*]

Hi Dad. What's up?

DAD: Hi Mae
How are you?

MAE: I miss you

DAD: I miss you, too
What did you do today?

MAE: I just bought some boots. They were the last ones in the store.
And they're not my size but they fit me!

DAD: That's good

MAE: What's going on?

DAD: I just wanted to—

MAE: Are you at work?

DAD: Well actually

[*The line goes quiet.*]

MAE: Hello—?

DAD: Well hold on here, I had a whole thing planned

MAE: Dad what's wrong?

DAD: I wanted to chat first and then—

[DAD's *voice breaks.*]

> I'm sorry, I thought I had myself together
> Why don't you tell me about your day?

MAE: Dad. What's wrong? You're freaking me out. Just tell me what's wrong

[DAD *tries to talk but he can't because he's crying. We hear only inarticulate sounds—just his attempt to speak and communicate despite great emotion. Not sobbing. It can be strange and alienating. Words trying to push through emotion and failing. Breath and the sound of his lips, saliva, tongue . . .*]

DAD [*some muffled cry, as if trying to say*]: They found it in my lungs.

MAE: I can't understand what you're saying.

DAD [*some muffled cry, as if trying to say*]: Sweetheart, they found it
    . . .

MAE: I'm sorry, Dad, I can't understand what you're saying.
    Do you want me to say what I think it is?
    Do you want me to say it for you?

DAD [*struggling*]:
    . . .
    . . .
    . . .
    It's in my lungs

MAE: Dad

DAD: And also—

[*He loses his voice again.*]

MAE: What did they say?

DAD:
    . . .
    . . .
    . . .
    . . .
    . . .
    . . .
    . . .
    Sweetheart . . .
    I'm sorry . . .
    I'm sahhh . . . .

[*Both of them trying to get their emotions in control in order to speak. Finally, finally, finally . . .*]

MAE: Dad? You still there?

DAD: Yeah, I'm here

MAE: Just give me a minute. I'm going to hang up. And then just give me a minute. And then I'm going to call you back.

•◆•

[*A breath and then brass. Sexy brass. Dance music. Pop music. It's* JENNY's *wedding. The siblings dance like you dance at a sibling's wedding—full of exuberance and joy, so drunk. They're sweating. Shirts get unbuttoned and shoes come off. Confetti is stuck to their sweaty foreheads. They dance. They dance. They dance. They dance. They dance in a circle.* HANNAH *does old jazz and ballet moves that she remembers from childhood. She points her feet. They dance.* JENNY *is shy and bobs up and down and claps her hands.* MATTHEW *sings along.* MAE *dances and looks at the floor. They dance. It's the last dance of the night. They know it's the last dance of the night and they dance like it's the last dance of the night.* DAD *is not there.*]

[*The music stops. The fluorescents pop on like a high school gymnasium. They stand for a moment. Sweaty. Covered in confetti. Looking at each other. We can hear them breathing.*]